What Makes A Christian Flaky?

A Simple Notation of Scriptural Disobedience and Cavalier Lifestyle Projected by So Many Who Claim to Have Identification With Jesus Christ, the Lord Of Glory

Robert E. Daley

The Larry Czerwonka Company, LLC
Hilo, Hawai‘i

Copyright © 2016 by Robert E. Daley
All rights reserved.

No part of this publication may be reproduced, stored in or introduced into a retrieval system, or transmitted, in any form, or by any means (electronic, mechanical, photocopying, recording, or otherwise), without the prior permission of the publisher. Requests for permission should be directed to permissions@thelarryczerwonkacompany.com, or mailed to Permissions, The Larry Czerwonka Company, 1102 Apono Place, Hilo, Hawaii 96720.

First Edition — June 2016

This book is set in 14-point Garamond

Published by: The Larry Czerwonka Company, LLC
czerwonkapublishing.com

Printed in the United States of America

ISBN: 069264282X
ISBN-13: 978-0692642825

Quantity Sales Discounts
Larry Czerwonka Company titles are available at significant quantity discounts when purchased in bulk for client gifts, sales promotions, and premiums. Special editions, including books with corporate logos, customized covers, and letters from the company or CEO printed in the front matter, as well as excerpts of existing books, can also be created in large quantities for special needs. For details and discount information contact: sales@thelarryczerwonkacompany.com

---

All scriptures used in this work are taken from the
King James Version of the Scriptures.

BOOKS BY **ROBERT E. DALEY**

A Case for "Threes"
A Simple Plan . . . of Immense Complexity
Armour, Weapons, And Warfare
from Everlasting to Everlasting
Killer Sex
Life or Death, Heaven or Hell, You Choose!
Raptures and Resurrections
Short Tales
So . . . What Happens to the Package?
Study and Interpretation of The Scriptures Made Simple
Surviving Destruction as A Human Being
The Gospel of John
The Gospel of John (Red Edition)
The League of The Immortals
The New Testament - Pauline Revelation
The New Testament - Pauline Revelation Companion
"The World That Then Was . . ." & The Genesis That Now Is
What Color Are You?
What Makes A Christian Flaky?
What Really Happened to Judas Iscariot?
Who YOU Are in Christ . . . RIGHT NOW!

The Enhancement Series

#1 Book of Ecclesiastes
#2 Book of Daniel
#3 Book of Romans
#4 Book of Galatians
#5 Book of Hebrews

The Deeper Things of God Series

#1 The Personage of God
#2 The Personage of Man
#3 The Personage of Christ

WHAT MAKES A CHRISTIAN FLAKY?

Introduction

It is the year 2016 A.D. Two thousand and sixteen calculated years have come and gone since Jesus Christ of Nazareth was physically alive and on the scene.

His death, and particularly his resurrection from the dead, is the pivotal point, and the fulcrum of balance, from Everlasting Past to Everlasting Future. What occurred at the time of Jesus' resurrection was calendar changing, and totally unprecedented within all of created time. And sad to say, it is still widely unknown, even unto this day.

At the resurrection of Jesus Christ of Nazareth nothing short of a brand new species of Human-Creation emerged. A Human-Being yes . . . but a Human-Being unlike any Human-Being that had ever been before him. A Super Human-Being. An Immortal, Super, Human-Being. A powerfully anointed, Immortal, Super, Human-Being. An authoritative, universe ruling, undefeatable, powerfully anointed, Immortal, Super, Human-Being.

There is no other created creature throughout the entire expanse of this Universe that is like unto this species that we belong to and called Homo Sapien. The risen Lord Jesus Christ is an unprecedented,

Super-charged, Immortal, authority-carrying, new prototype example of Homo Sapien.

And he has opened the Immortal-Portal, and cut the trail, for any person on this planet that would care to follow him into the uncharted regions of eternity.

The initiating criteria for membership into this elite constituency is a Spiritual-Rebirth. But it does not simply stop there. For this program to be eternally valid for any individual, there must be recognition of the truth and a willingness to obey the simple, limited rules that apply. Today, acknowledgment and understanding of those requirements are sorely lacking, at the very least, within the Western Hemisphere. This little work addresses some of the *flaky* notions and mental disorders that people have who today call themselves *Christians*.

But before we actually address various categories, let us have an understanding that there are extreme and varying degrees of *flakiness*. Let us also understand as well, that if any individual does not qualify for full *flakiness* status in every category, that does not mean that they are exempt and not potentially *flaky* in certain other areas. Truthfully speaking, all *Christians* currently living on this planet do qualify for being *flaky*, in any area that they depart from Scriptural accuracy and spiritual truth, even if they are revered **icons** within *Christendom* and vehemently declare of themselves that, **"we see."** *(John 9:41)*

A fact of reality is that a woman is either pregnant or not pregnant at any given moment in time . . . there is no middle ground. So it will also be with baseline spiritual truth. The Scripture does not give any of us the liberty of being able to pick and choose what we want to believe and then obey, or what we do not want to believe and then not obey. And in any given area of life that an individual chooses to not believe, or to not obey what the God of mercy and grace has declared and established within His written word . . . then they are *flaky*.

Contents

1. Terminology — **1**
2. Truth — **7**
3. Holiness — **14**
4. Righteousness — **20**
5. Obedience — **27**
6. Attitude — **33**
7. Genuine Love — **37**
8. Stewardship — **41**
9. Relationships — **55**
10. And So? — **60**

Terminology

CHAPTER 1

"Now this I say, that every one of you saith, I am of Paul; and I am of Apollos; and I am of Cephas; and I am of Christ." (I Corinthians 1:12; Enhanced)

Spiritually speaking, on this planet, we have people who call themselves Baptists. Other individuals call themselves Methodists. Still others are referenced as Lutherans, Pentecostals, Russian Orthodox, Catholics, Greek Orthodox, Episcopalians, Ana Baptists, Mormons, Jehovah Witnesses, Congregationalists, and on and on and on it goes. And all of these constituents consider themselves to be *Christians*. The Bible says,

"Jesus answered and said unto him, Verily, verily, I say unto thee, Except a man be Born-Again, he cannot see the Kingdom of God."
(John 3:3; Enhanced)

"Jesus answered, Verily, verily, I say unto thee, Except a man be born of water and of the Holy Spirit, he cannot enter into the Kingdom of God."
(John 3:5; Enhanced)

*". . . Now if any man have not the Holy **Spirit of Christ, he is none of his.**"* (Romans 8:9b; Enhanced)

The new Spiritual Rebirth that has been made available by the resurrection of Jesus Christ of Nazareth, and the discussion of an individual becoming **Born-Again**, has acutely come to the forefront, terminology wise, within the last few decades at the very least. The absolute necessity for **all** individuals on the face of the planet to become Born-Again within their spirit is established within the declaration that Jesus of Nazareth made to Nicodemus, the Jewish Pharisee, and is not a frivolous suggestion but is rather a mandate.

The criteria for the New-Birth is given unto us by the Apostle Paul in his letter to the believers at Rome.

***"For within the heart a man believeth unto righteousness; and with the mouth confession is made unto salvation** of a man's spirit."*
(Romans 10:10; Enhanced)

To ***"believeth unto righteousness"*** in layman's terms means to trust fully in the risen New Creation Jesus Christ of Nazareth to be your personal Savior, not in word only, but also in reality. And to accept that he Spiritually Died for you so that you could Spiritually Live for him *(II Corinthians 5:15)*. It is not simply an acknowledgment of his existence and validity or an acceptance of him as the *Savior of the world*. He must become YOUR own personal Savior.

The previously titled constituencies that we have noted are more commonly known by the vast majority of peoples on this planet as different *religions*, or *denominations* of religion. Now an accurate definition of *religion* is: *"A designated set of rules and regulations by which men attempt to contact, and then have dealings with, the Living God"*. And the only genuine religion that this world has ever seen is the religion of Judaism, because God is the One who gave the rules and regulations to the Nation of Israel in the first place. All other religions, worldwide, have their set of rules and regulations given to them by men. And additionally, any religion is going to be found to carry very little weight when a person ultimately stands before the living God.

Within all of the different *groups* of people that we have mentioned, who label themselves as *Christians*, there are specific individuals within each of these *groups* that are Spiritually Born-Again. But all of these different *groups* of people go to church. All of those church-goers are not necessarily genuine *Christians* even though they may think that they are. The Spiritual Re-Birth is the determining and deciding bottom-line factor.

People who go to church, simply to fulfill an unstated obligation, and then call themselves

Christians . . . but are not truly Born-Again within their spirit, are spiritually *flaky*.

People who believe that the specific *group* that they belong to is the only true *group* that God is speaking unto, and working with, within the Earth today . . . or that theirs is the one true *group* that will assure them an entrance into heaven . . . are spiritually *flaky*.

People who may be genuinely Born-Again, and believe that they know God, but are persuaded that they do not have to go to any particular local church and submit themselves unto the instruction and guidance of a local pastor, because they are *independent agents*, or have an independent calling on their lives, and hear from and receive their instructions directly from God Himself . . . are spiritually *flaky*.

And none of these people can present a Biblically solid case for their persuasion or position. In addition, none of these people believe or even think about the fact that they are spiritually *flaky*. They are sincere people and are fully persuaded concerning their convictions. And they may be socially very nice individuals; gregarious and outgoing; happy in attitude and seemingly excited about the things of God. But they are quite limited in their personal knowledge of what the word of God actually declares, and have drawn their own conclusions concerning various Biblical requirements in the different areas of life. In the long run, these people are not an asset to the established Body of Christ on the Earth today, but rather are a liability. And that is because their lives affect so many other lives that they come into contact with. And these other people, particularly those who are young in the Lord, observe these *independent agents* and are adversely influenced into believing that it will be perfectly alright with God if they choose to run off and do the same thing.

There is an authorized Spiritual-Governmental-Structure that the Head of the Church established shortly after he returned to heaven *(Ephesians 4:11)*. Even though that reality is not being strictly adhered to within *Christendom*, we do have established local churches everywhere, with pastors in place that are there for the purpose of feeding and protecting the sheep . . . not just some of the sheep but all of the sheep.

Do these various people purpose to be *flaky*? No, probably not. Do these certain individuals really desire to influence other people to become *flaky*? No, probably not. The difficulty is that they are grossly, spiritually, under-educated themselves. The Bible declares,

> **"My people**, *which are called by my name*, **are destroyed for lack of knowledge. And because thou hast rejected knowledge, I will also reject thee."** *(Hosea 4:6a; Enhanced)*

Notice that the Bible does *not* say that the people of God are destroyed for a lack of zealousness. And they are *not* destroyed for a lack of good intentions, or for a lack of conferences or seminars, or for a lack of prayer, or for a lack of compassion, or for a lack of anything other than a *lack of knowledge*.

And spiritual insight testifies that the Scripturally referenced knowledge, spoken of in the verse above, does not normally come from simply attending church on Sunday mornings, or from regular, standard, routine, mediocre, or middle-of-the-road Bible studies. A few favorite memorized Scriptures, or a general working knowledge of the passed-on-down-the-road traditions of men, is not enough. Nor is a doctrinal position that has been passed down from generation to generation, and many times is erroneous, going to be enough either. There needs to be a further pressing into the deeper things that God has for us. And that requires time and focus on the Word of God with a willingness to abandon anything that is not the truth as presented within the Scriptures. We must receive the testimony of the One who really knows what the truth is, on any given subject. The Holy Spirit has promised to lead us into all truth if we are willing to receive it. The question becomes, are we?

Truth

CHAPTER 2

"Then said Jesus to those Jews which believed on him, If ye continue in my word, then are ye my disciples indeed;

And ye shall know the truth, and the truth shall make you free." (John 8:31-32)

"Sanctify them through thy truth: thy word is truth." (John 17:17)

The entire content-basis of all known Truth, is found within the established written Word of God. The Bible. The Scriptures. The Holy Spirit inspired, 3-D encoded, *"incorruptible seed"* of the Word of God. (I Peter 1:23)

"According as his divine power hath given unto us all things that pertain unto life and godliness, through the knowledge of him that hath called us to glory and virtue:" (II Peter 1:3)

"For the prophecy came not in old time by the will of man: but holy men of God spake as they were moved by the Holy Ghost." (II Peter 1:21)

What an individual person *experiences* is not necessarily the Truth. It is indeed real, but that does not make it the Truth. The established report of the Lord is the declared Truth *(John 17:17)*. Reports from all other sources, even though we may have personally *experienced* it, if they conflict with the report of the Lord, are definitively false. Again, that does not mean that they are not quite real. They are indeed real, and they do exist, and there are manifestations that accompany these reports, but they are not the Truth if they conflict with, or are in opposition to, the declarations of the written Word of God.

Sadly, that is not an accepted axiom among a majority of the people on this planet, including *Christians*. And additionally as sad, is the reality that there are intelligent men and women who declare that they have spiritual insight, and proceed further to influence multitudes of other individuals, and profess that ***"we see"*** *(John 9:40-41),* and yet they are limited concerning spiritual depth, insight, and harmony with Truth.

There is singularly, only one Truth. In any given situation, within any of the three Realms of Existence that we have any dealings with, no matter what may be happening, even right before our very own eyes and ears, or how loud it may be shouting to arrest our attention, there is only one Truth. *". . . **thy word is truth**" (John 17:17).* So *anything* that is contrary to the Word of God, in any way, is not the Truth.

> *"Forever, O Lord, thy word is settled in heaven."*
> *(Psalms 119:89)*

The very first thing that occurred after Adam and Eve's creation, and within the Garden of Eden, was that the Word of God came under assault from the powers of darkness.

> *"Yea, hath God said . . ."* *(Genesis 3:1)*

Satan knew full well what God has said. Yet he purposed to twist that which had been declared in order to promote his insidious lie. Eve fell prey to the subtlety of the serpent *(I Timothy 2:14)* and influenced Adam to follow her lead *(Genesis 3:6)*. The **Law of Sin** was given legal entrance back into this world, to operate for the second time *(Romans 5:12)*, and has kept Mankind in spiritual bondage and servitude ever since.

After centuries of patience and persistence, the declared and now written Word of God, has been Divinely 3-D encoded into this world by the Holy Spirit of God. Today, the same encoding Holy Spirit of God provides the decoding keys for the understanding of spiritual Truth. And intellectual intelligence is not the baseline criteria. God declares, and has given unto Mankind, the option to believe the Truth or to not believe it. And the very actions that will follow an individual, do indeed speak louder than words, and certainly will testify as to what a man truly believes. Whatever a man ultimately believes will affect his Everlasting Future, and will leave him either in harmony with God or in opposition to Him. And as it is with all opposition, it cannot be allowed to run free and adversely affect the remainder of the harmonious creation; it must be contained. *(Matthew 25:41)*

The desire of all Born-Again children of the Most High God should be to know the Truth on any given subject, mainly because of the liberation that comes with it. However, that is not usually the case. So many *Christians* **think** that they know the Truth and that they **know** what the Bible says, but in reality, they do not know. They are so fully persuaded concerning what they personally think that they will argue and fuss, and get upset and pout, when they are challenged and confronted with the Truth, and usually will declare *"show me that in the Bible!,"* as though God's directive concerning personal study:

"Whom shall he teach knowledge? And whom shall he make to understand doctrine? Them that are weaned from the milk, and drawn from the breasts.

For precept must be upon precept, precept upon precept; line upon line, line upon line; here a little, and there a little:" *(Isaiah 28:9-10)*

> *"But the word of the Lord was unto them precept upon precept; precept upon precept; line upon line, line upon line; here a little and there a little; that they might go, and fall backward, and be broken, and snared, and taken."* (Isaiah 28:13)

does not apply to them, and they want it to be laid out 1 – 2 - 3, A – B - C, right before their very eyes. *Flaky!* They are too lazy to study. It takes too much effort to study. They do not have time to study. To them, just the regular reading of the Bible is considered studying, and they have already studied enough.

The God of all creation does not change *(Malachi 3:6)*. The word that He has spoken does not change *(Psalms 119:89)*. The ways in which He works do not change *(Proverbs 8:32)*. The power that He possesses, and has demonstrated, does not change *(Revelation 19:6)*. The established truths of reality do not change. And men are the ones who had better change if they desire to spend Eternity with the One whose initial and everlasting love for them does not change.

The Scriptural Truth Of **These** Matters Is This:

* All angels were created with a free-will. *There was an active Social Order on planet Earth, long before Adam was created. *There are *Other Creatures* within God's universe that are not angels and they are not men. *The serpent in the Garden of Eden was not the devil Satan. *There are but three active Realms of Existence in operation. *If you are not spiritually Born-Again, and you physically die, you will go directly to Hell. *There are only three active conditions or States of Death. *God the Father is not God the Son; and God the Son is not God the Holy Spirit; and God the Holy Spirit is not God the Father. *If you are a New Creation *in Christ*, then you are not a Jew anymore . . . God does not make hybrids. *Tithing is mandated for all covenant people of God, and it is not open for discussion. If one does not tithe, then they are classified as a thief. *Jesus paid the full debt that sickness and disease demands and one does not have to be sick ever again for as long as they live. *Your spirit and your soul are not the same things. *Jesus died spiritually as well as physically. *The Law of Moses was given only to the Nation of Israel. *Jesus was not born in the month of December. *If you are spiritually Born-Again, then you cannot sin in your spirit anymore. *ptsChristians* are not obligated to live by the Ten Commandments. *Jesus did not know that he was a member of the Godhead until he was twelve years old. *For a *Christian*, generational-curses do not apply. *The Wise Men were not visitors to the shelter at the birth of Jesus. *You can be spiritually Born-Again and still go to Hell when you die. *Demons cannot fly. *There is no such thing as reincarnation. *Christians* cannot be demon possessed. *Evolution is a lie straight from the Pit of Hell. *Jesus, who is indeed God, will remain a Man as well, forever. *All genuine *Christians* shall become Immortal. *Global Warming is a blatant lie because men cannot destroy what they did not create in the first place. *The womb of a Human woman is the doorway between two worlds. *Every *Christian* has the responsibility to save their own soul. *God will not send anyone to Hell. *Judas Iscariot lived through the crucifixion of Jesus, was spiritually Born-Again, and yet went to Hell.

Are we upset yet? Is this author considered a heretic? Is your blood percolating, and are your emotions enflamed? Then your soul is again running amok even now. Is it time to throw this little book away?

Well, before you run off in a huff, Scripturally DISPROVE any of the above points of notation. And if you really want to **know** the Bible, study out what the Word of God has to say on any, or all, of these outrageous statements.

Holiness

CHAPTER 3

Holy: (of a person) living of spiritual purity; (of things) dedicated, set apart, for sacred usage. -- As taken from the New Lexicon Webster's Dictionary of the English Language.

"For I am the Lord your God. Ye shall therefore sanctify yourselves, and ye shall be holy; for I am holy:" *(Leviticus 11:44a; Enhanced)*

"Because it is written, Be ye holy; for I am holy." *(I Peter 1:16)*

God is a Person that is spiritually pure, unto the absolute. The Bible tells us that God is Light, and in Him is no darkness at all *(I John 1:5)*. There is no stain of Sin connected to His Being. There is no filthiness attached to Him in any aspect; there are no nuances of that which is inappropriate, operating within Him. And there is nothing negative whatsoever concerning His Personage. By way of a visual example, He is as pure as the newly driven snow.

God's original divine design was to create other beings that are intelligent, and are free-thinking, and are as holy even as He is holy. In their origin, all angels were created to be loyal, and holy. In their origin, all *Other*

Creatures were created to be loyal, and holy. In his origin, Man was created to be loyal, and holy. So . . . what happened?

The creation of, and the bringing forth of, the **Law of Sin** is what happened.

Iniquity is the ***bud*** of evil. It is the mating together of renegade thoughts, with inappropriate personal desires. Iniquity starts the ball of rebellion rolling on the inside of an individual *(Isaiah 14:12-14)*. At any given point in time, should that ***bud*** of iniquity be given any license or place, a conception of Sin will be the end result. When iniquity and spoken words conceive, and proceed to merge together with established foundational laws, a creation will occur *(Proverbs 16:30)*. In like manner, when iniquity and action in line with that iniquity conceives, with an ultimate merging together with established foundational laws, a creation will occur. And that creation is not something that is going to be coming forth from God. The author of the **Law of Sin** is the once-upon-a-time holy angel, named Lucifer *(Ezekiel 28:13-15)*. Iniquity ***budded*** forth from within him *(Isaiah 14:13-14; Ezekiel 28:15)*, and he did not deal with that iniquity at the outset *(Acts 8:22)*. Because he did not spiritually deal with the iniquity, he eventually acted upon that very iniquity *(Ezekiel 28:16)*, and the heinousness of Sin creatively burst forth onto the scene as a spiritual **Law** *(Romans 8:2)*. The workings of the **Law of Sin**, and true holiness are diametrically opposite one to the other. Should one be able to provide a viable solution to the **Law of Sin** dilemma, one will then be able to definitively require holiness, instead of simply suggesting it.

For the bulk of Mankind, specifically during the seven-thousand-year Probationary Period on this planet, the **Law of Sin** and its workings will deceive, and devastate, and ultimately destroy to the uttermost. God has provided a viable solution to the "Sin-Problem" for all individuals who would enter into a covenantal relationship with Him. The solution began with a man named Abram, and the Abrahamic Blood Covenant, and will conclude with a man named Jesus Christ of Nazareth and the Christian Blood Covenant. For any believing Abrahamic Blood Covenant persons, belonging to the Nation of Israel, before the crucifixion of Christ Jesus, the consequence of Sin and the penalty that accompanies rebellion was remitted with the resurrection of the Lord Jesus Christ. For individuals from all other nations of the globe, and including the Nation of Israel, the "Sin-Problem" solution for the spirit of a Man became a manifested reality with that same resurrection of Jesus, and the bringing forth of the Christian Blood Covenant. The current beneficiaries of the Abrahamic Blood Covenant solution are all in heaven today, having been taken there by Jesus Christ of Nazareth after his resurrection *(Ephesians 4:8)*. And in this day in which we live, the remainder of the Abrahamic Blood Covenant people that make up the Nation of Israel, will never get to benefit from the "Sin-Problem" solution because of their rejection of Jesus the Christ. They will still maintain their position of being in an Abrahamic Blood Covenant relationship with God . . . but they will also remain in a *dead-in-their-sins* spiritual condition, always.

The reality of entering into the Christian Blood Covenant, and the remission of the "Sin-Problem" within a Man's spirit, is still an open invitation issue to whosoever. By the grace of God, both Jews and Gentiles from all over the globe are responding to the preaching of the Gospel. Acceptance of the "Sin-Problem" solution, *(John 3:3,5)* through Christ Jesus, severs all legalities that Sin once held over any given individual *(II Corinthians 5:17-18)*. The power of God is now available for these Christian Blood Covenant individuals to *"perfect holiness in the fear of the Lord" (II Corinthians 7:1)*. Should any person professing a relationship with a Holy God, choose to walk in unholiness, they are *flaky*. Should they willingly continue in the bondage of the lust of the flesh, and the lust of the eyes, and the pride of life *(I John 2:16)*, then they are *flaky*. Should they choose to remain carnally minded, as a child-of-God, *(Romans 8:6)* then they are *flaky*.

God, the Father of His covenant family, is spiritually pure. The children of the Family of God are to be spiritually pure as well, just like their Father. The Father has set a standard, and made power available, through the indwelling of His Holy Spirit, for His family members to become spiritually pure *(Philippians 4:13)*. To whatever degree we ignore what God has made available, and do not avail ourselves of the power, and think that we can just do it on our own; or, are not really that interested in seriously dealing with fleshly things, we are *flaky*. God is an adult, and though we are currently His natural children, we are supposed to grow up and become a spiritual adult as well. To just *Cadillac* through this life, and not press into the spiritual realities of holiness, is not wise. *"I'm a good person, and I'm living the best that I know how"* may not be good enough. What, of that which is unholy, do we allow our eyes to gaze upon? What, of that which is unholy, do we allow our ears to listen to? What, of that which is unholy, do we intermingle with? We know that it is not right down deep within our heart. What, of that which is unholy, do we allow to utter forth from our lips, through ignorance, emotional outbursts, and naiveté? What part of **"be ye holy, because I am holy"**, do we not understand? *(I Peter 1:16)* Should we think that simply bearing the name of *Christian* grants us the liberty to think, and to talk, and to act like all of the other individuals who are in the world around us, then we are *flaky*.

"For unto whomsoever much is given, of him shall be much required" *(Luke 12:48).*

And, please believe this author when he says that we will be required to account for that which we have been given. Holiness is not an *out-of-reach* issue. God has laid the ground work and done all of the hard parts, we simply need to stop loving Sin so much.

Righteousness

CHAPTER 4

"For he hath made him to be Sin for us, who knew no sin himself; that we might be made the righteousness of God in him." (II Corinthians 5:21; Enhanced)

The Greek meaning of the word *righteous*, or the condition of *righteousness* within the Strong's Concordance reference work, is that of a state of *Innocent, Holy, Just, and Right*.

The God of all creation is Himself Innocent, and Holy, and Just, and Right. And every intelligent, moral, free-willed creature that the loving Creator has brought forth into existence has been without flaw in their original creation condition. They have been created perfect in every aspect of their being. They were Innocent, Holy, Just, and Right.

At some point in time, in the days gone by, the worst possible thing that could have ever happened occurred. That which we know of and refer to as the **Law of Sin** burst forth into existence and onto the scene.

Had it not been for the entrance and operation of this spiritual *short circuit* within the whole of God's creation, we would find ourselves living in a perfect world, which would be part of the collection of perfect star systems that would be operating in their fullness within a perfect Universe. But, ultimately that is not what happened.

For the person not familiar with the Scriptural revelation of what the element of the **Law of Sin** is, a layman's summation, in common, understandable terminology, might be: *Any thought, or word, or deed that is issued forth, contrary to and against, that which is known to be right and true.* Sin is also an abject hatred of all that is good and holy. And, Sin is the very foundation of any and all rebellion, against any type of established authority. Involvement with Sin depicts a full-force dealing with of the heinousness of death, and the ramification of death, in any and all of its conditions or states. And, Sin is a proliferation of spiritual darkness affecting every nook and cranny of the three Realms of Existence . . . Thought, Word, and Deed.

Because of Sin and the evil power of what Sin affects, from the days of Adam and Eve, all men have been guilty, and unholy, and unjust, and not right before God. *(Romans 5:12)* The nature and character of men has been a Sin polluted and defiled character, and their nature has been altered and become Human/Satanic, and there is nothing that any man can do about it.

And we are not talking about whether a person is *nice* or not. An individual with a Sin-polluted, defiled nature and character can still be a *nice* person. But when the chips are down, and the extreme pressure is applied, the true inner nature of their character will begin to seep out and emerge, and they will ultimately turn out to be not very *nice* at all.

Because of Sin, men have been declared guilty as they stand before God right from the very first man. God's original design was that men rule over the whole of what He has created *(Hebrews 2:8)*. How is that going to work as it should, if men are unholy and not right at their very core? How are they going to be able to decree a proper and correct decision, if they are unjust? How are they going to render a working of innocence, if they are all guilty? It cannot be done.

When we look at the subject of righteousness, whether within the Old Testament account or the New Testament account, we need to understand that within each account, there is an established Blood Covenant that is put into place . . . and the issue of righteousness that goes with each Covenant, in each account, is a two-edged sword issue. Side A of the sword blade is the *Legal Aspect*, and side B of the sword blade is the *Behavioral Aspect*.

Within the Abrahamic Blood Covenant, which is the established Covenant of the Old Testament account, the side A *Legal Aspect*, is credited righteousness that God gave unto Abraham and to all of his descendants. This originates within the Blood Covenant walk that we find in Genesis chapter fifteen. Abraham does not directly walk through the corridor of blood with God, but rather is on the sidelines asleep *(Genesis 15:12)*, but he is credited as if he had personally walked through the blood. If the person is a legitimate participant of the Abrahamic Blood Covenant, by being able to trace their lineage back through Jacob, and back through Isaac, and unto Abraham, then they are credited as being *Legally* righteous.

Within the Abrahamic Blood Covenant, the side B *Behavioral Aspect* is established within the **Law of Moses**, and the innocent animal, sacrificial system *repair kit* that went with that **Law**.

"Again, When a righteous man doth turn from his righteousness, and commit iniquity, and I lay a stumblingblock before him, he shall die. Because thou hast not given him warning, he shall die in his sin, and his righteousness which he hath done shall not be remembered; but his blood will I require at thine hand." *(Ezekiel 3:20)*

The **Law of Moses** provided a basis for behavioral righteousness, and any breach of that **Law** was able to be effectively dealt with, and repaired, through the shedding of innocent animal blood for the guilty

Human-Being. Credited *Legality*, combined with behavioral obedience, produced a *righteous* condition for any individual within the Nation of Israel.

Within the Christian Blood Covenant, which is the established Second Covenant of the New Testament account, *(Hebrews 10:9)* the side A *Legal Aspect*, is the reality of being *in Christ (Romans 8:1)*. This also originates within the Blood Covenant walk that we find within Genesis chapter fifteen, in which the pre-incarnate *Burning Lamp*, Second Person of the Godhead did indeed walk through the corridor of blood with the First Person of the Godhead *Smoking Furnace (Genesis 15:17)*. If a person is a legitimate participant of the Christian Blood Covenant, by being Born-Again, *(John 3:3,5)* and being *in Christ*, then they *Legally* become the very righteousness of God Himself. *(II Corinthians 5:21)*

Within the Christian Blood Covenant, the side B *Behavioral Aspect* is established by obedience to the Royal Law. *(James 2:8)*

"Little children, let no man deceive you: he that doeth righteousness is righteous, even as he is righteous." *(I John 3:7)*

"In this the children of God are manifest, and the children of the devil. Whosoever doeth not righteousness is not of God, neither he that loveth not his brother:" *(I John 3:10)*

Righteous *Legality* reality, combined with behavioral obedience, produces a *righteous* condition for any individual within the Body of Christ.

Flaky Christians violate the above Scripture all of the time. *Flaky Christians* lie, and cheat, and steal, and blaspheme, and commit fornication, and abuse their purchased bodies with modern *art*, and alcohol, and cigarettes, and drugs. Their language of choice is often questionable, and when they are confronted with these violations, they are ready with their *"valid excuse"* for why they are struggling with these issues, and yet never seemingly able to come to a place of resolve. They attempt to postpone the judgment of reality, but shall never be able to escape the consequences, except through a genuine repentance and a quality decision that will result in **"sorrow that needeth not to be repented of"** *(II Corinthians 7:10)*. In reality, they deny the finished work of the cross and are currently interested in continuing to fulfill the soulish desires of the mind and of the body. They are *flaky*. And sadly, many times they have been genuinely graced with a legitimate gift from God, and they have done good things. They really believe that they are spiritual, and as such, could never ever possibly be *flaky*. And all of this *flakiness* is, for the most part, overlooked by the Body of Christ and relegated to the category of *"well, it ain't no big deal brother,"* because there is such a profound profusion of disobedience in operation. This is especially true within Western Christendom.

Righteousness is the standard that God has set into place. Christians are not *Natural* individuals anymore. Because of the finished work of the cross, they have become Supernatural in legality and have been blessed with the power from on high to overcome this world and all of the shortcomings within it. *(Philippians 4:13)* Should we choose to abide and operate at a level of convenience and comfortability, then we best come to the realization that we are *flaky*. This is **not** a game. This is Life and Death. And the Scriptures reveal that God is not too happy with our continuing to play around with Death.

Obedience

CHAPTER 5

"And Samuel said, Hath the Lord as great delight in burnt offerings and sacrifices, as in obeying the voice of the Lord? Behold, to obey is better than sacrifice, and to hearken than the fat of rams."
(I Samuel 15:22)

Obedience is diametrically opposite of disobedience. It is important to bring that reality to light because, concerning this particular issue of obedience, there is no gray area or middle ground. A person is either obedient or they are disobedient, just as a woman is either pregnant or she is not pregnant. *"Well, I'm not a perfect person"* is usually the statement of excuse that is made to justify disobedience. And, it is indeed a true statement. There has been only one perfect person thus far, and that is the Lord Jesus Christ of Nazareth. But the statement is made because of conviction within the heart and is used in an attempt to justify speech or actions that are already known to be wrong.

However, there is such a thing as disobedience by way of ignorance. Not knowing, or being aware of the right thing to do, and as such, disobeying unwittingly.

Eve was the first person to be actively disobedient without really knowing what was happening . . . she was deceived *(I Timothy 2:14)*. Adam did not teach her all that she should have been taught, and Satan found a crack in her spiritual make-up that he could take advantage of, using the most subtle of all of the beasts of the field *(Genesis 3:1)*. The **Law of Sin** is the instrument that made men disobedient in the first place. *(Romans 6:16)* And up until the time of Moses, two-thousand plus years into the program, there was no *instrument* available to assist men in *"knowing"* what was right and what was wrong. They simply did what they wanted to do, and were moved by what they thought was best at the time. But they were still captives to the **Law of Sin** all along.

The Scripture tells us that Jesus is the light ***"which lighteth every man that cometh into the world"*** *(John 1:9)*, so we know that God has given unto men a conscience to steer them in the right direction, concerning their behavior. But that conscience can be seared with a hot iron through disobedience, and the gentle direction from a loving God ignored, in order to achieve and fulfill the current desire or passion.

Once God was in a Blood Covenant relationship with men, He was the One who became potentially guilty of having complicity in the matter, because He does know better. Because of the covenant, he is responsible for protecting His people from harm. So, when the Nation of Israel grew to a substantial size, God gave unto them an *instrument of behavioral modification* known of as the **Law of Moses**. This **Law** informed them that ***"Thou shalt not . . . , Thou shalt not . . . ,*** and ***Thou shalt not."*** *(Exodus 20:1-17)* And even though they had the ***Law***, they still disobeyed because of the driving force and power of the **Law of Sin**. *(Romans 7:15-23)* So, God gave unto them a spiritual *repair kit* in the form of an innocent animal sacrificial system, for when they *blew* a spiritual tire. The blood of an innocent animal would pay for the guilt of a ***Law*** breaking Human-Being, whenever a breach occurred. And up until the resurrection of the Lord Jesus Christ from the spiritual and physical dead, that was all that covenant men could do.

However, today it is a completely different story altogether. The resurrection of Jesus Christ makes all the difference in the world. Jesus took care of the "Sin-Problem" for me. The debt that I owed has been paid, and the shackles of my bondage have been broken.

"For sin shall not have dominion over you: for ye are not under the Law, but under grace."
(Romans 6:14; Enhanced)

"Who hath delivered us from the power of darkness, and hath translated us into the kingdom of his dear Son:" *(Colossians 1:13)*

For those that are *in Christ*, we now belong to another kingdom, with a whole new set of guidelines to go by *(Colossians 1:13)*. In Christ, I am now spiritually redeemed *(Galatians 3:13)*. In Christ, I am now more than a conqueror *(Romans 8:37)*. In Christ, I am now seated at the Right Hand of God my Father *(Ephesians 1:20)*. In Christ, my spirit is now sealed by the Holy Spirit of God *(Ephesians 1:13)*. And, the **Law of Sin** cannot affect my spirit anymore *(I John 3:9)*. I now can do all things . . . through Christ, which strengtheneth me *(Philippians 4:13)*. So, to cut to the chase, excuses for blatant disobedience no longer carry any validity with God. I am not a captive to the **Law of Sin** any longer *(Romans 6:14)*, and the power of Christ-in-me will help me to learn, and to obey the word of my God.

I am not to swear or use bad language anymore *(Ephesians 5:4)*. I am to take inappropriate thoughts captive to the obedience of Christ utilizing the weapons of my warfare *(II Corinthians 10:5)*. I am to be a doer of the word of my God, and not a hearer only, deceiving myself *(James 1:22)*. I am to cleanse myself of all soulish and physical filthiness *(II Corinthians 7:1)*. I am to lay aside every weight, and the sin which doth so easily beset me, and run my course with patience, looking unto Jesus, who is the author and finisher of my faith *(Hebrews 12:1-2)*. I am to put off, concerning the former conversation, the old man, and put on the new man, which is created in righteousness and true holiness *(Ephesians 4:22-24)*. And if I consciously, knowingly, and willingly refuse to do these various things . . . then I am *flaky*.

"Well, Pastor Rob, that sounds pretty severe." Oh really? God has done all of the hard parts, and broken the power of Sin, and we continue to say through our behavior that, *"I don't really care what you did, I still want to continue in my sin."* How many years does it take to make, and act on a quality decision? How many years does it take to effect change? *"Well, Pastor Rob, I'm working on it."* No, you're not. You are lying, first to God and then to yourself. You still choose to dwell on those foul thoughts, don't you? You still choose to say those inappropriate words, don't you? You still choose to continue with those abominable actions, don't you? You are not *"working on it"* at all because you still want to do those things, and you simply continue to do them . . . again, and again, and again, and again. Do you really believe that any of the lame excuses that we put forth for continued disobedience are going to hold any validity with God?

And what are we doing to the rest of the Body of Christ? How are we adversely influencing young Christians? What kind of a testimony does our life's routine reflect? Are we willing to be honest about these things, or do we pretend that we are talking about somebody else? Because lemmings follow one another over the cliff, shall we simply excuse what we are doing, because someone else is doing it? Where is the integrity? Where is the individual obedience to what the Word of God is telling us to do?

Behavioral obedience is probably the major problem that exists within the Body of Christ today. And, make no mistake about it . . . it is a problem of *flakiness*. Possibly not all-out *flakiness*, but *flakiness* never the less.

The Bible tells us that God prefers obedience above sacrifice; *(I Samuel 15:22)* and it is worth pondering just how much we impress God with our gospel projects and "good works," if we are not going to obey His simple instruction of obedience in the first place. It is clear that changes need to be made, because without any changes . . . there will be no change. May we purpose to not procrastinate any longer. Stop the disobedience right now, and begin acting upon the instructions that we have in the Word of God.

Attitude

CHAPTER 6

"For as he thinketh in his heart, so is he . . ."
(Proverbs 23:7a)

We will find out in the end that it really does all begin with attitude. An infant Human-Being is a bundle of warm clay that is ripe for molding. There is no such thing as *innocence* with newborns because **"all have sinned and come short of the glory of God"** right from the womb. *(Romans 6:23)* But there is not a more appropriate time to begin to have a positive effect on the shaping of a brand new Human-Being than during infancy.

Now, for people who are yet part of the constituency of *the world*, this is really a moot point. They are dead in their sins, and the newborn child they have recently produced is dead in its sin as well. *(Romans 5:12)* During the growth process of the child, in the natural setting, the chances of instruction and guidance from the source of truth, the Word of God, are slim to none. Nevertheless, attitudes will begin to formulate based upon existing parental-attitude influence and personal desire fulfillment of the child as it grows. And, the *ways of the world* will be actively projected all around them, and they will begin to build themselves their own personal perspective and attitude . . . toward God, toward other people whom they personally know, toward other people whom they do not personally know, and even toward the circumstances of life's issues and activities. Unfortunately, most of those attitudes will sadly turn out to be *bad attitudes*, because that is what Sin does.

However, if we are talking about a household that professes a genuine knowledge of, and an active walking with, the Personage of the One True God, then that should not be the case. *Christians* have the benefit of liberty from the power of Sin, if they obey God *(Romans 6:14)*. *Christians* have the position and power of prayer and petition unto the One who is able to deliver and protect them to the uttermost. *Christians* have weaponry of a supernatural nature to the casting down of Satanic strongholds *(II Corinthians 10:4)*. *Christians* have a tremendous advantage over the people of *the world*. But sadly, too many times, *Christians* are lazy. Unless they have renewed their mind, and cleansed themselves of soulish filth, and have definitively put away active sinning, they may still have a *bad attitude*, and will not do what is necessary for the benefit of the brand-new child.

Christians are supposed to train up the child in the **"nurture and admonition of the Lord"**. *(Ephesians 6:4)* But too many times what they do is simply bring the child to the church. The church is expected to teach them, not me. The church is expected to positively affect them, not me. I have my own set of *problems* that I am dealing with, and I do not have the time. Sounds very much like a problem of *attitude* does it not? And any *attitude* that is without adjustment is going to be *flaky*. That does not mean that the person is necessarily 100% *flaky*, but to the extent that they continue with a *bad attitude* in any venue, they are *flaky*.

Flaky attitudes many times lead to personal *snits*. *Flaky* attitudes usually contribute to producing emotional *poutiness*. *Flaky* attitudes lead to *schisms* between both natural and spiritual family members. *Flaky* attitudes reflect a *"this is the way that we have always done it"* mindset. *Flaky* attitudes project an *"I want it my way"* declaration. *Flaky* attitudes are not a benefit or an asset to the Body of Christ. *Flaky* attitudes have a direct connection to spiritual carnality and they emanate straight from Hell.

Attitude adjustment is absolutely necessary for anyone who claims a connection with Christ Jesus. When we hear the declaration of *"more of Jesus and less of me,"* it is supposed to be much more than just a clever statement. And when it comes right down to it, my *attitude* adjustment is going to be strictly up to me. Should I profess that I know Jesus personally, and also, that I am a child of the Living God, and then not submit myself therefore unto God and with His help deal with my *attitude*, then I am *flaky* (James 4:7). And we are not talking about allowing ourselves the liberty of something that continues on for years and years and years before it is dealt with. We have a responsibility before God to become the type of children that He would like us to be. *Attitudes* will have a direct effect on obedience. *Attitudes* will have a direct effect on behavioral righteousness. *Attitudes* will have a direct effect on genuine love. *Attitudes* will have a direct effect on stewardship. *Attitudes* will have a direct effect on every single area of our lives. And *bad attitudes* will not be acceptable to the God of grace. If we have a *bad attitude* and are *flaky*, we should avail ourselves before it is too late, of God's abundant mercy and grace. Dealing with our *attitude* is a primary necessity.

Genuine Love

CHAPTER 7

"He that loveth not knoweth not God; for God is love." (I John 4:8)

The Personage of God Himself is the very basis for genuine love. He is the God who has *cut the trail* for all of creation. His love is an unchanging and faithful love, and His commitment to that love extends unto the uttermost. The Scriptures paint a gloriously clear picture within their pages:

"God exhibits extended endurance, and is gentle in His dealings with His creation. God is not envious at any time, of anyone or anything. God does not inappropriately promote Himself, and is not egotistical. He does not behave Himself in a denigrative manner, and is not self-centered. He is not easily angered, and does not allow any evil thoughts to come forth. He does not rejoice in renegade thoughts or inappropriate personal desires, but does rejoice tremendously in the truth. He bears all things patiently. He believes in all things good. His hope is undaunted, and He endures unto the uttermost. He never fails." (I Corinthians 13:4-8a; Paraphrased)

Here on this Earth, we erroneously think that we know all about what love is. Our heartstrings of compassion are moved in light of obvious need, and we yearn earnestly for everything to work out all right. The person that one may be attracted to pledges faithfulness forevermore, and we melt with the consoling expression of unbroken commitment. Our lusts rise to a crescendo of emotional desire and we interpret that to be a sign of fidelity and unwavering love. We declare with seeming sincerity that *"I love you"* and expect a response of obedience to unspoken physical urges and hormonal promptings. And where is the real genuinity?

When the *circumstances* do not fall precisely into place as anticipated, we are gone in less than a heartbeat. When the *loved one* does not live up to all of the expectations that we have, we abandon our place and position in short order. When the *niceness* dissipates on either side of the fence, the evil growling from within wipes the smile from off of our faces. And when I cannot get what I want to fulfill my desire and lust, bitterness causes the stain of disdain and contempt to pollute my professed sincere *love*.

Love is not a *feeling*, love is a Person. Love incarnated into flesh and became Jewish Jesus of Nazareth. Love walked among men without blaming and condemning. Love endured all that Hell could throw at him, both on the Earth and under the Earth. Love allowed the heinousness of evil to capture him and plunge him into the depths of hopelessness. Love was willing to *take the hit* on the behalf of all who would consider the exchange. Love ultimately emerged victorious, never to be challenged by darkness again.

Love has offered a gift. *"Find your life in me"* rings true for all who will. In Christ, we have become intertwined with victory and success. In Christ complete strength and provision is assured. In Christ immortality and superiority is promised. There are no longer any limits to anything. **"Nothing shall be impossible"** (Matthew 17:20). All things can be done. There is nothing that is *"too hard."* And the eons ahead speak of a tapestry of manifest love oozing from every fiber.

It is the today-of-now that presents the difficulty. Our focused goal should be *"more of Jesus, and less of me"* with each passing day. And when we profess a connection with Love Himself, and obstinately continue in our *selfishness* in whatever capacity of life's issues, then we are *flaky*. Self-less-ness is the desired goal. Jesus of Nazareth was the most self-less Human-Being that has ever come forth and walked on this planet. He should be our personal hero. He should be the very one we want to emulate. So, what is stopping us . . . ???our continual mantra of Me, Me, Me, Me. That is why we are *flaky*. Do not be deceived. And stop the denial. We are *flaky* when it comes to genuine love and we know it. But it does not have to stay that way. We can begin to put *J*esus first, *O*thers next, and *Y*ourself last, and experience the *JOY* that will come forth when we do. Love always emanates with a gentle outward flow and never allows the current to shift. Love is for others, and if it is genuine, then reciprocity will occur because **"love never fails"** *(I Corinthians 13:8).* The very basis for all of life is love, and even though at this point in time, we really fall short in our full understanding, nevertheless the eons ahead will ripple with the melodic notes of love, oozing forth from every pore of creation.

Stewardship

CHAPTER 8

"And he said also unto his disciples, There was a certain rich man, which had a steward. And the same was accused unto him that he had wasted his goods.

And he called him, and said unto him, How is it that I hear this of thee? Give *now* an account of thy stewardship; for thou mayest be no longer *my* steward.

Then the steward said within himself, What shall I do? For my Lord taketh away from me the stewardship. I cannot dig *and* to beg I am ashamed.

I am resolved what to do, that, when I am put out of the stewardship, they may receive me into their houses.

So he called every one of his lord's debtors unto him, and said unto the first, how much owest thou unto my lord?

And he said, A hundred measures of oil. And he said unto him, Take thy bill, and sit down quickly, and write fifty.

Then said he to another, And how much owest thou? And he said, A hundred measures of wheat.

And he said unto him, Take thy bill, and write fourscore.

And the lord commended the unjust steward, because he had done wisely; for the children of this world are in their generation wiser than the children of light.

And I say unto you, Make to yourselves friends of the mammon of unrighteousness; that, when ye fail, they may receive you into everlasting habitations.

He that is faithful in that which is least is faithful also in much. And he that is unjust in the least is unjust also in much.

If therefore ye have not been faithful in the unrighteous mammon of this world, who will commit unto your trust the true riches?

And if ye have not been faithful in that which is another man's, who shall give unto you that which is your own?

No servant can serve two masters. For either he will hate the one, and love the other; or else he will hold to the one, and despise the other. Ye cannot serve God and mammon." (Luke 16:1-13; Enhanced)

Stewardship is a covenant issue and is ultimately a combination of honesty, faithfulness, and righteous behavior. At a point in time, the Nation of Israel was given a set of *rules* which they were to live by, called the **Law of Moses**. These *rules* are contained within the book that we call the Bible. Within the nuances of the established set of *rules*, God elaborated on the subject of money or the medium-of-exchange of a given region. Additionally, these *rules* were not open to, nor subject for, discussion amongst whom they were given to . . . and the Jewish people did not get to vote on whether to accept them or not. They were decreed by God, and that meant that they became mandatory.

Also, these *rules* were not a matter of *rocket science*. In simple layman's terms:

- It was accepted that all gifts, talents, and abilities, were a grant by God the Creator, to any given individual.
- That individual could then exchange these gifts, talents, and abilities, in the areas of farming, or fishing, or husbandry, or building, or some other various labor endeavor, for compensation in the accepted medium-of-exchange.
- Monetary resources, or an increase of the herd, or fruitfulness of the harvest, or plentifulness of the *catch*, were all products that emanated forth from the gifts, talents, and abilities that were granted by the Creator.

- Of the total increase of the varied products, ten percent was declared as belonging to the Lord God, who gave the gifts, talents, and abilities in the first place. That was his *fee* for His services rendered. That *fee* is Biblically known of as the *tithe*. And what was to be done with the *tithe* once it left the hand of the individual was not open to suggestion by those who returned the *tithe*. That was God's business and His responsibility.
- However, failure to return the required *tithe fee* classified the individual as a thief, incurred a further 20% penalty of indebtedness, opened the door for the devil to kill, and destroy, and steal from the individual. And hindered the work of promoting righteousness and salvation potential to people not in a covenant relationship with the God of Creation.

There are other nuances and details concerning benevolence for the poor, and provision for the brethren within the covenant, and certain National obligations as well, but they are minor compared to the standard mandatory *tithe* doctrine that was established.

Today, that same set of **Law of Moses** *rules* that were given to the Nation of Israel are no longer legally valid for enforcement, concerning the New Creation

Body of Christ Project, because the person of Jesus of Nazareth fulfilled them all, within his finished work on the cross of Calvary. However, because the *rule* of the *tithe* was established by God the Creator 430 years before the **Law of Moses** *rules* were given, it still does remain very much valid for New Creation Body of Christ covenant individuals, even unto today.

Within 21st Century Christianity, individuals that do not *tithe* to their local church are dishonest, poor stewards, and they are *flaky*. All *excuses* that are given for not *tithing* are simply invalid. All *good reasons* that are given for not *tithing* are additionally invalid. All *scripturally-based* protests that are given by *spiritually-knowledgeable Christians* are invalid as well. If an individual who proclaims to be a genuine *Christian* does not return unto the local spiritual *storehouse* that which belongs to their God in the first place, then they are dishonest and manifestly *flaky*.

Additionally, if an individual is a declared *"minister of the gospel,"* and receives *tithe* resources from other individuals who are sitting under their instruction, and they do not *tithe*, then they are dishonest, unfaithful, and manifestly *flaky*. And if an individual is a declared *"minister of the gospel,"* and is the recipient of the *tithe* resources that are given by others, and he or she *tithes* to their own ministry and hence receives the *tithe* resource from themselves, then they are dishonest, poor stewards, and manifestly *flaky*.

Brothers and sisters, we are talking about Scriptural truths and spiritual realities here, not the money. God is not the loser when men do not adhere to spiritual truths and purpose to operate dishonestly. It is the very men themselves that are the losers. And to even think that these issues do not carry that much importance, and attempt to dismiss them as insignificant, is *flaky* thinking.

* * *

In addition to the *tithe* issue, the local church is currently the ordained locale for spiritual instruction and growth, for one who claims to be a *Christian* today. There are 168 calculated hours within a standard week of *time*. Of those 168 hours, approximately 6-7 hours of attendance at the local church would normally be asked for those who say that they want to learn about eternal things. And if we are talking about the Sunday attendance alone, then less than 3 hours would be the average commitment. Faithfulness to spiritual instruction in these closing years on planet Earth is at a dismal all-time low. The Bible says that men will be lovers of pleasures more than lovers of God *(II Timothy 3:4)*. They usually have places to go, and people to see, and things to do . . . but those places and things do not include God. And what might understandably be the real reason for this acute faithlessness? Spiritual *flakiness*. However, in the Scripture, it is referred to as a *lukewarm* condition. *(Revelation 3:15)*

"I was sooo tired this past Sunday Pastor Rob . . . My friend came in to visit me from out of town . . . I did not have enough gasoline to get there . . . I was not feeling very well . . . Opps! I overslept . . . I just forgot all about it . . . I had someplace else that I really needed to go . . . My family is here, and I usually do not get to spend much time with them . . . I just cannot handle those other Christians, they are such hypocrites . . . I had church alone . . ." And on, and on, and on it goes. Persons who claim that they are genuine *Christians*, and have an established hit-and-miss attendance record at the local church, or who do not attend church very much at all, are sadly just plain *flaky*, and that is the truth of the matter.

They come and they cry that their relatives need the Lord, but they manifestly demonstrate that attendance to things of God is not really that important to them . . . and then they wonder why their loved ones remain distant from the Lord. Why don't we simply stop the wimpy excuses, the lies, the denials, and the justifications for exhibited *flakiness*. Why don't we simply own up to it, and call a spade a spade. Even though the Bible does not specifically say that you have to go to church, where else might we receive any kind of credible spiritual instruction? *(Hebrews 10:25)* Wal-Mart? The beach? The Mall? At home? From my friends? The internet? From a DVD? Or do we think that we are already knowledgeable enough?

And if I do go to a church, and someone says something, or does something, that *"bends my little feelers"* . . . do I just run away? *"I'm not going to go to that church anymore because they hurt my feelings!" "I don't agree with what the pastor says anymore!" "They just don't see it the way that I do!"* . . . And when these issues arise, am I willing to discuss the situation with the pastor? Am I willing to inform the pastor that I am leaving the church because of *"differences"* that have arisen? Am I willing to try and work out any anomalies that there might be, in what was said or done? No! I quickly pick up my *bag* of issues and take them to another church down the street where, truthfully, I can cause the same problems that I have just left. *And* that is what proves that I am genuinely *flaky*. I'm just gone in 60 seconds.

* * *

Again, as a *Christian*, should I happen to tell you that I am going to call you sometime, or that I will come over and visit you, or that we will go somewhere and do something together, or that I will be right back after I take care of something pressing, or some other issue that I verbally pledge myself to do . . . and then I promptly abandon my pledge without even giving it so much as a second thought, then I am *flaky*. Not that there are not some very legitimate exceptions. However, it would seem that in this current day and age in which we live, our personal word of commitment is not really worth very much.

And within my own identified thinking, the validated reason for my behavior is that I have found, through experience, that the word of other individuals around me is not worth very much either. And sadly, when it ultimately comes to even believing what God tells me in the Scripture . . . because I seem to be surrounded by liars and have become a manifest liar myself, God must be a liar in the things that He says within His word. How sad! Where will it all end? When are we going to be willing to stop this infantile behavior??? We are individuals that are physically full-grown, and we love to prove it every chance that we get. . . . We are individuals that profess that we are mentally full-grown, and we jump to any challenge to the contrary. . . . Are we so spiritually ignorant as to think that we can continue in these described immature behaviors and still consider ourselves spiritually full-grown? *FLAKY!!* God help us.

Is it really too late to gird up our loins? Are we truly past the point of no return? Can't we see how much we are hung-up on the Almighty Self? You tell me. And if these few stated issues are really not as they have been presented, then this author must be living on a different planet, and he will need to repent immediately.

* * *

Additionally, as a *Christian,* I petition other believers to supply me with money, or furniture, or appliances, or clothing, or other items of *necessity,* because, through adverse circumstances, I find myself destitute, and back at square-one. I cannot go to the *world* concerning my needs, because the *world* does not have the love of God, and will probably tell me to take-a-hike. But believers in the Lord Jesus are supposed to be kind, and loving, and compassionate, and willing to help those that need a leg-up. And please do not misunderstand . . . there are genuinely legitimate times that this scenario occurs, and that it is quite valid . . . but a revolving door of this type of situation is usually the end result of *flakiness.* Even though it is not recognized, it is normally driven by the Devil. And one of the express purposes of Hell is to suck completely dry the resources of the average man or woman of God, that is struggling with whatever of their own needs that they may have, and cause that the problem that existed with one, is now exacerbated to include how many more than one?

And inflamed emotions of *compassion* are the perfect tool to utilize to facilitate this financial draining. And since these persons have come to the Household of Faith for assistance, at this point in time the question that should be posed is: Is the impoverished person seeking after the *"things above"* as a baseline of their life?

(Colossians 3:1) For instance, does the impoverished person attend a local church on a regular basis? *(Hebrews 10:25)* Does the impoverished person tithe? *(Malachi 3:10)* Does the impoverished person exercise good stewardship over the resources that come into their hands? *(Colossians 3:23)* And do not even try and tell this author that they are destitute and really have *nothing*. In this day of entitlements, everybody has some kind of revenue available to them on a regular basis, even if it is small. What are they doing with that provision? Are they open to sound counsel? Whatever happened to the last refrigerator that they received free? Whatever happened to the last pieces of furniture, or clothing, or other appliances, or the cash money that was placed in their hands? How much of that money might have gone to pay for alcohol? Or to pay for tobacco? Or to pay for drugs? Why is this person impoverished in the first place? How did they get into this kind of a condition? Manifested *flakiness* in their *Christian* approach to life, that is how. They have decided long ago that they know best . . . no one can really tell them anything . . . they march to the beat of a different drum . . . they are smart, and know what they are doing . . . so, they start out on their own path of travel, and over a designated period of time, here they are at the doorstep.

Now, obviously, this author is callous and hardhearted and without feeling. He has very little, or no, compassion operating within him, and is indifferent to the *needs* and the *sufferings* of his fellow-brethren. Right? Brothers and sisters, there is a real-life war going on all around us. And we find ourselves right in the middle of it. Light is being assaulted by darkness. Truth is being assaulted by lies. Things above are being challenged by the things of this Earth. So, whose report are we going to believe? When are we going to be willing to deal with the real problems at hand, instead of just throwing resources at the symptoms?

* * *

Finally, as a *Christian* brother, should I need to borrow a tool from you, or an item or article of your personal possession and you are gracious enough to loan it to me . . . should I lose it, or break it, or damage it somehow, or it gets stolen while it is in my possession, the normal 21st Century *Christian's* response is usually: *"Oh! I'm sorry"*, and that is the last that you will hear about the matter. The actual thought of repair of the item, or replacement for that which is now gone, does not even occur in our thinking. *Flaky*. Concerning honesty and stewardship . . . *flaky*. And please, again, do not misunderstand, these examples are not always the case; but, they are usually the rule and not the exception. Within the Scriptures, we receive the report of the Lord on what should happen. The examples that we may look at were with the Nation of Israel it is true, but have the principles really changed just because we belong to a Gentile nation?

Replacement or restitution within specific Scriptural instances was five-fold *(Exodus 22:1)*, or sometimes four-fold *(Luke 19:8)*, or, at least, times two. Courtesy and common sense would dictate that we would, at least, replace what was lost or damaged or broken or stolen while it was under our care and genuinely part of our stewardship responsibility.

Where is integrity in our *Christian* society today, and within the days in which we live? Do we even know what the word *integrity* means anymore? Where is genuine honesty? Where is established faithfulness? Where is unwavering loyalty? Where are the word and action accountability? Are these stated subjects still realities, or have they morphed over into the arena of concepts? Within *Christianity* they certainly do not seem to be the rule, but do they still even have some sort of place within the category of exceptions? And, once again, the irrefutable proof of these questions is where?

This author believes that it is more than time to take an inventory of our spiritual condition, and then choose to act upon what the Holy Spirit of God will reveal. Time is running very short. The shout will take place quite soon, and the Lord Jesus will issue the upward call before we know it. It is not too late, but it can no longer be postponed. Make the decision today to stop making excuses and attempts at justification, and bring the areas of *flakiness* to a halt. God will be more than happy to help.

Relationships

CHAPTER 9

"Submitting yourselves in love one to another in the fear of God.
Wives, submit yourselves unto your own husbands, as *you would* **unto the Lord."**
(Ephesians 5:21-22; Enhanced)

"Husbands, *purpose to* **love your wives, even as Christ also loved the church, and** *he laid down his life, and* **gave** *all of* **himself for it;"** *(Ephesians 5:25; Enhanced)*

Sounds quite idyllic, does it not? In this world in which we live, it is no surprise that the *"Battle of the Sexes"* continues to rage on *(Genesis 3:16)*. Since the fall of Adam and Eve, because of Sin's effect upon Mankind, the woman has steadily declined in position, esteem, and seeming importance. The female figure is frequently, even unto today, exalted, promoted, lusted after, nakedly displayed, hormonally pursued, exploited, denigrated, demeaned, and treated as if it were nothing more than an unresponsive blow-up doll. In many cases, a God-class-compliment of the Express Image of the Creator *(Hebrews 1:3)*, is looked upon as little more than a piece of chattel property. And men, created *in* the image, and *after* the likeness of a Holy, Righteous, and Pure God, behave like a common dog concerning one of the most miraculous gifts ever bestowed upon creation . . . the independent granting of bringing forth another God-class, forever-to-be-in-existence, potential ruler of this Universe, at the discretion of the two-shall-be-made-one couple. *(Genesis 2:7; Ephesians 5:31)*

Satan recognized the value of the woman as being the God-designed doorway, through which one must pass to enter into this world, and carry the full thrust of given authority over all of the handiwork of God's hands *(Genesis 1:26; Psalms 8:4-6; Hebrews 2:8)*. Unredeemable *half-fallen-angel* and *half-sin-stained Human* children *(Genesis 6:2,4)*, coming into existence would be just the ticket to foil the prophecy of a Redeemer for the world of Mankind. *(Genesis 3:15)*

However, today, for one who professes an identification with the living God, and the source of all Light *(I John 1:7)*, to continue to actively walk within the veil of darkness that he has just left behind, is to be sure, *flaky*. For a *Christian* husband to lord it over his wife, and to treat her like she is his personal slave, is *flaky*. For that same man to expect his wife to be at his every beck-and-call, and to satisfy his every whim, is also *flaky*. For his behavior to be such, that his wife is too afraid to speak up and say anything to anybody concerning that behavior, is an outright shame to his credit. It also brings a reproach upon the name of Christ, whom he says that he represents, and is indeed *flaky*. His heavenly mandated responsibility is to guard her against potential evil, to guide her in a gentle instruc-tive manner, and to love her as Christ loves the church, and gave himself for it. *(Ephesians 5:25)*

For any *Christian* man to think that women are not considered valid in the eyes of God when it comes to any preaching or teaching ministry or witnessing opportunity, is also *flaky* thinking, and a yielding to of false doctrine. The risen Jesus of Nazareth is the gender equalizer *(Galatians 3:28)*, and the commission to go into all the world and preach and teach is given to all believers. *(Matthew 28:20; Mark 16:15)*

For *Christian boyfriends* to allow themselves to be moved into a temptation situation, where they are willing to compromise the purity of their *girlfriend*, for the fulfillment of their own personal lust, is *flaky*. For them to be Biblically ignorant, and believe that there is no real moral guideline for behavior in place and that they can act upon bodily urges of *"love"* without any consequence, is more than *flaky*, it is stupid *(I Corinthians 6:18-19)*. Gross immorality is currently operating within the Body of Christ among young people of today, and Hell is anxiously waiting for the ticking clock to run out of time. And the professed excuse of *"Pastor Rob, we're in love"* is completely invalid and holds no water. Sin is sin.

And disobedience is disobedience. And both of them give evidence of, and display, *Christian flakiness.*

There is no such thing as *Christian-Life-Partners,* nor of *Christian-Significant-Others,* nor of *Recreational-Sex* within this New Way. All of those declarations are man-made abominations, and invalid before the eyes of a Holy God. Covenant is what God established for legality purposes, and without a Marriage Blood Covenant in place between a man and a woman, there is no sexual exchange allowed . . . at all . . . period.

Christian women who attempt to *rule* over their husbands because they have the more dominate personality can be *flaky.* Women have been designed by God to respond, within the Marriage Covenant; and even if they have been compelled to move into a headship position through divorce or abandonment, should they enter again into a Marriage Covenant, they are again admonished to respond rather than reign.

The *"Feminist Movement"* within the United States of America is a Hellish institution. The very pretext is founded in rebellion. It is anti-Biblical and designed to disrupt and destroy the original male-female progression-to-family basis. *"I don't need anyone"* would accurately apply as a mantra.

Christian girlfriends that just cannot wait to grow up and use their bodies are *flaky.* Eagerly willing to move into the temptation situation themselves, they use their bubbling hormones to stimulate the natural drive within their *boyfriends*. The pressure from projected media within the world around us today is staggering that is true, but that is no excuse. Professed identification with Christ, combined with a willing ignorance of Scriptural declaration, blended with worldly influence and unrestricted raging hormones... equaling, disobedience is *flaky*.

For Christianity, God has called us to a higher standard level of living. Accepting Jesus Christ as our personal savior is more than just a *get-out-of-Hell-free* card. And if we approach our walk with God frivolously, and continue to live a cavalier lifestyle, then we are *flaky*, and the consequences could be devastating.

The subject of men with men, or women with women, will not even be discussed as it is so obviously against God's purposes!

"Examine yourselves, *as to* **whether ye be in the faith** *or not*; **prove your own selves. Know ye not your own selves, how that Jesus Christ is in you, except ye be**have as **reprobates?"**
(II Corinthians 13:5; Enhanced)

We would do well to pay heed to Scriptural admonition.

And So?

CHAPTER 10

The eons that yet lay ahead will be punctuated by Human perfection concerning the adopted children of the Most High God. The *conforming-to-the-image-of-Christ* (Romans 8:29) process will be completed, and the New Creation men and women that make up the constituency of reigning sovereigns shall think, and talk, and act, just like the risen Jesus of Nazareth, their captain. Individual uniqueness and personalities shall remain fully intact for every New Creation person, but the current *more-of-Jesus-and-less-of-me* declaration will have become a moot point. All thoughts that independently emanate forth from glorified heirs of salvation will be processed by the power of the Holy Spirit, unto the obedience of Christ. All words that are selected to be uttered by children of the Most High God will be pleasant to the ear and filled with life. All actions that are to be undertaken by immortal youngsters of the Divine will be in absolute harmony with the perfect aspect of the one will of the Living God (Romans 12:2). There will not even be one opportunity for *flakiness* of any kind, because of the perfection that the Holy Spirit of Grace will effect within all members of the Body of Christ.

The Millennial Reign of the Lord Jesus will afford one-thousand years of on-the-job training for the saints of God *(I Corinthians 6:2-3)*. We will have been resurrected from the dead, or caught up to meet the Lord in the air *(I Thessalonians 4:16-17)*, or as in some cases, will even have experienced personal martyrdom *(Revelation 6:9)*. But that unpleasantness is over now and living within the locale of the immortal *(I Corinthians 15:53)*, we shall be ruling and reigning with Christ Jesus our Lord. Fallen principalities, powers, rulers of the darkness of this world, and spiritual wickedness in high places, *(Ephesians 6:12)* will be subject to the righteous judgment that we shall be assigned by Christ Jesus to declare *(I Corinthians 6:3)*. Demons and their operations will come to a screaming halt, and they shall also hear the decree of condemnation, and experience the anguish of plunging into a molten Lake of Fire. Natural men and women in Terrestrial Bodies, who are the inhabitants of planet Earth, are still Spiritually Dead in their sins and technically mortal. They will be living under the watchful eye of a governmental iron-rule *(Revelation 2:27)*. Within the final millennia of probation, they will discover whether or not they will be able to enter into the Everlasting with the God of love *(I Corinthians 6:2)*. New Creation saints will be the determining factors of influence concerning that issue. And throughout the whole of the time-frame allowance, all thought, word, and deed realities of the members of the household of

God will be transitioning into perfection by willful submission to the gracious Holy Spirit of God.

It is here on this Earth, and it is within the time frame of right now, in the 21st Century, that the severe lack of self-discipline problem exists, amongst those who are called believers. Within the extended future ahead, there are **no** *flaky Christians* operating within the universal everlasting, and abiding with God. Within the comparatively near future just ahead, there are **no** *flaky Christians* operating on the Earth, within the Millennial Reign of Christ Jesus. Sadly, we find the true reality of genuine *flakiness*, right here and right now. And why is that?

Is it impossible to discipline ourselves? Are we really not able to reign in our thoughts . . . or do we simply choose not to, because they may be much too enjoyable? Are we really not able to curb our tongue . . . or do we continue to choose not to, because it releases selfish weight-on-our-will pressure, and really conveys what we feel? *(And besides, they deserve it!)* Are we really not able to stop acting so badly, in so many different ways . . . or do we knowingly, willingly, and consciously choose not to change how we act *(or react)*, because that would indeed require some effort on our part, and we really are just too lazy to deal with it?

Why do we tend to think that changes to our thoughts, or changes to our words, or changes to our actions are automatically just supposed to happen as time simply ticks by? Are we so foolish as to believe that just because I chose to accept Jesus of Nazareth as my personal savior, that now the Holy Spirit will work it so that I wake-up one morning and it will all be different? I do not have to discipline myself, to actively deal with those foul thoughts that find their way into my mind? I do not have to discipline myself to zip-the-lip and shut my big mouth because I feel that I just really need to tell-it-like-it-is? I do not need to discipline myself, concerning my bad behavior? *"After all, Pastor Rob, I love God, and Jesus is my Lord [Luke 6:46], so everything else will just take care of itself?"* Will it really? You might want to read those Scriptures again. The truth of the matter is that without any changes, there will be no change.

We have mentioned previously within this work, concerning that self-rationalization statement, *"Well, I am only Human and not a perfect person"* . . . is a verbal justification of any and all of life's issues that we refuse to confront. And even today, during a beautiful wedding ceremony, this author heard the usage of our *"Human weaknesses"* interwoven into the very vows that were being exchanged. May this author ask . . . if Adam and Eve had not fallen prey to the seduction of Sin, what *"Human weaknesses"* would we now have? Additionally, Jesus of Nazareth is a Human-Being . . . so what *"Human weaknesses"* did he have when he was walking among men? You see, in all honesty, all of our *"Human weaknesses"* are a consummate adding-up of our willingness to yield to Sin. And in Christ Jesus, because of his finished work on the cross, we have been freed from the compelling power that Sin exercises *(Romans 6:14)*. So that pretty much takes all of the wind out of the sails of our excuses, does it not?

And so . . . the real bottom-line is that we are empowered by our God to be more than conquerors, *(Romans 8:37)* and to not be *flaky* anymore. We should be men and women who refuse to fall for the seductions of the enemy. Men and women who are determined to press in unto excellence in every endeavor of our lives. Men and women who will choose to rise to the challenge of living for *him. (II Corinthians 5:15)*

The work has been done. The strength has been given. The *ball* is now in our court. Take the challenge, make the decision, and follow it through to victory and success. And start doing it today!

Maranatha! He will be here in a blink.

Meet the Author

By-The-Book Ministries, Inc. began in 2001 as a teaching outreach. Rob E. Daley has been gifted by God to be able to explain biblical truths in an easy to understand manner.

Many have been blessed by his teaching style.

Rob was saved and filled with the Holy Spirit in 1978 and has been instructed by the greatest teacher of all—the Spirit of Truth Himself. Rob is an ordained minister with the Assemblies of God International Fellowship and has pastored in various churches over the past 34 years.

It is the desire of this ministry to see the body of Christ solidly taught, and grow up into the things of the Lord. Rob is available for seminars, retreats, conventions, etc.

Rob can be reached at:

thedaleys@bythebookministries.org

http://robdaleyauthor.com

www.ingramcontent.com/pod-product-compliance
Lightning Source LLC
Chambersburg PA
CBHW032211040426
42449CB00005B/547